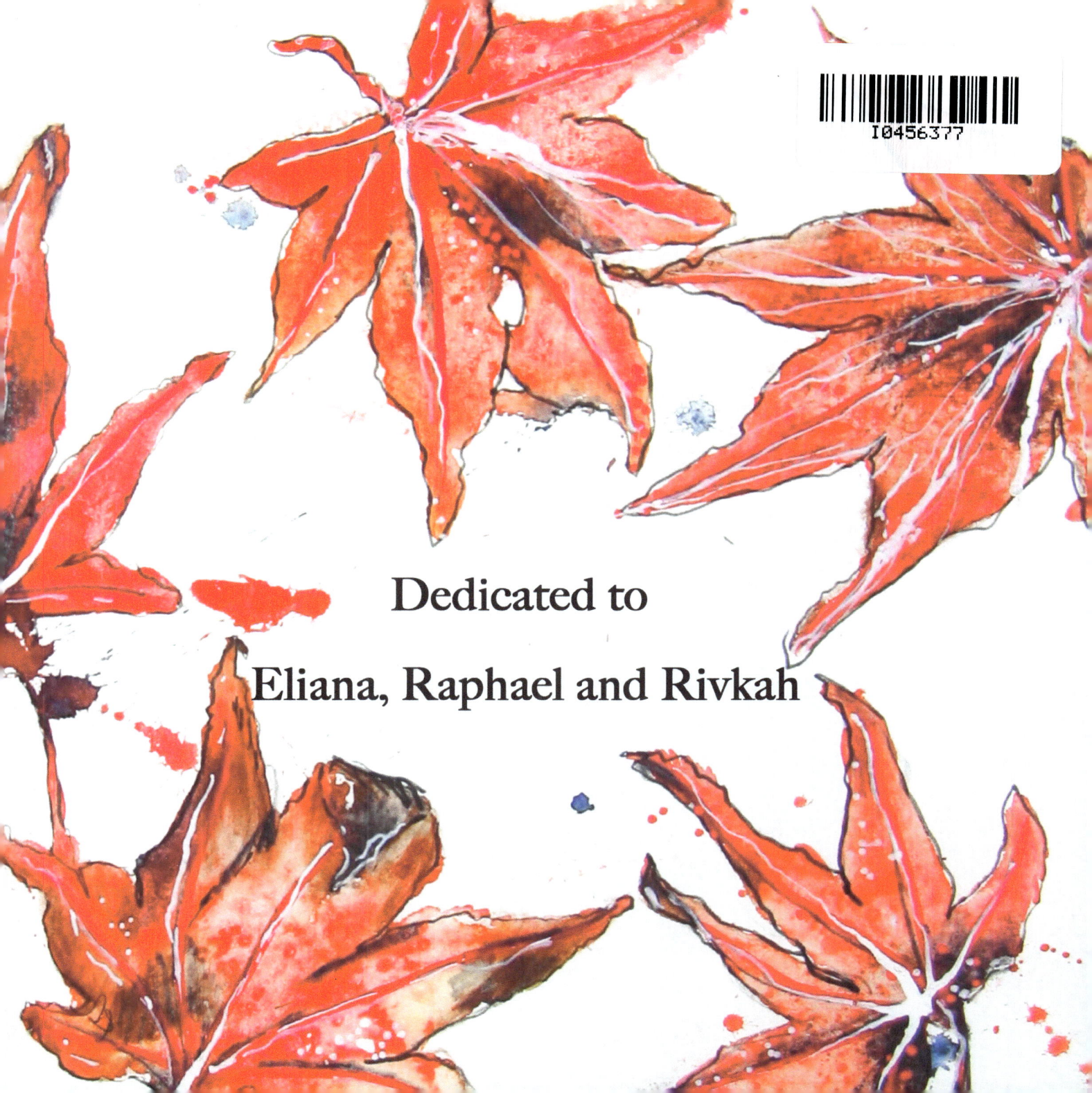

Dedicated to

Eliana, Raphael and Rivkah

How Majestic is Your Name,

When I look at the heavens, the work of your fingers,
the moon and the stars,
which you have set in place,
what is man that you are mindful of him,
and the son of man that you care for Him?

Psalm 8:3-4

Puddle Hunt

Rebecca Morris

It's raining, it's pouring, puddles have started forming,

Rain coats
on,

welly boots
on,

it's time to
go

exploring!

Pitter, patter,
splish, splosh, splatter!
There's a puddle, a great green puddle,

Mummy, can we jump in?

OH, YES!

But where have we gone?
How did this happen?
We've slipped through into
another world!

People as tall as Christmas trees,

Rainbows as high as the eye can see!

This is fun,

Such good fun!

Pitter Patter, splish, splot, splatter

It's starting to rain again!

There's a puddle,
a deep, gold puddle,
Come on, let's jump in!

Oh, YEH!

Whizz,

Bang,

Flashes
of
light!

Rolls of
thunder,

We're at
Bonfire
night!

Smokey, burning fragrance
in the air,

Glory and wonder everywhere!

This is fun!
Such good fun!

PUMPKIN SPICE

PARKIN

TREACLE
TOFFEE

TOFFEE APPLES

BABYCINO

Pitter patter, SPLISH, SPLOSH, SPLATTER!
It's starting to rain again!

See that puddle, a fiery red
puddle...
Hold hands tight,
It's very bright!

Spinning,
whirling,
whooshing,
turning,
up into the whirlwinds
we fly!

Unicorns twirling on carousels,
Sparkling torrents of light ringing bells!

This is fun!

Such good fun!

Pitter, patter, splish, splosh, splatter,
Here comes the rain again!

There's a puddle...
A gigantic puddle,

Let's jump in!

Oh yeh!!!

Hold your breath, we've plunged into the depths,

where narwhals swim and dolphins play!

A deep, mysterious place,
Where ancient treasures lay!

This is fun!

Such good fun!

Pitter, patter, SPLISH, SPLOSH, SPLATTER

It's starting to rain again.

There's a puddle... a kaleidoscope puddle,

Are you ready to jump in?

Pure bliss!

Out we shoot,

On the tail of a star!

I know where we
are.

There's the Earth,
so tiny below,

and there are the
planets,

so beautiful,

see how they
glow!

We look so big
and the Earth
looks so small,

We have
nothing
to fear at all!

Through the helter skelter spiral to the ground.

The rain has stopped, the sun is shining bright...

Shall we go on another adventure tonight?

Treasure hunt check list

Compass (proverbs 8:27)
Face/ vault of the deep (Genesis 1)
Windows (Matt 6:22)
Menorah (Exodus 25)
Harp (Psalm 33:2)
Treasure (Matt 6:19-21)
Scroll (Revelation 5)
Portals (John 10:9)
Leaves (Revelation 22:2)
Rainbows (Revelation 4:3)
Whirlwinds (Ezekiel 1:4)
All consuming fire (Deut 4:24)
Christmas tree (John 15)
Lion (Revelation 5:5)
Door (John 10:9)
Above the circle of the earth (Isaiah 40:22)
Tent (Isaiah 40:22)
Unicorns (Numbers 24:8)
Helter skelter (Genesis 28:12)
Night time (Psalm 119:148)
Fortress (Psalm 18)

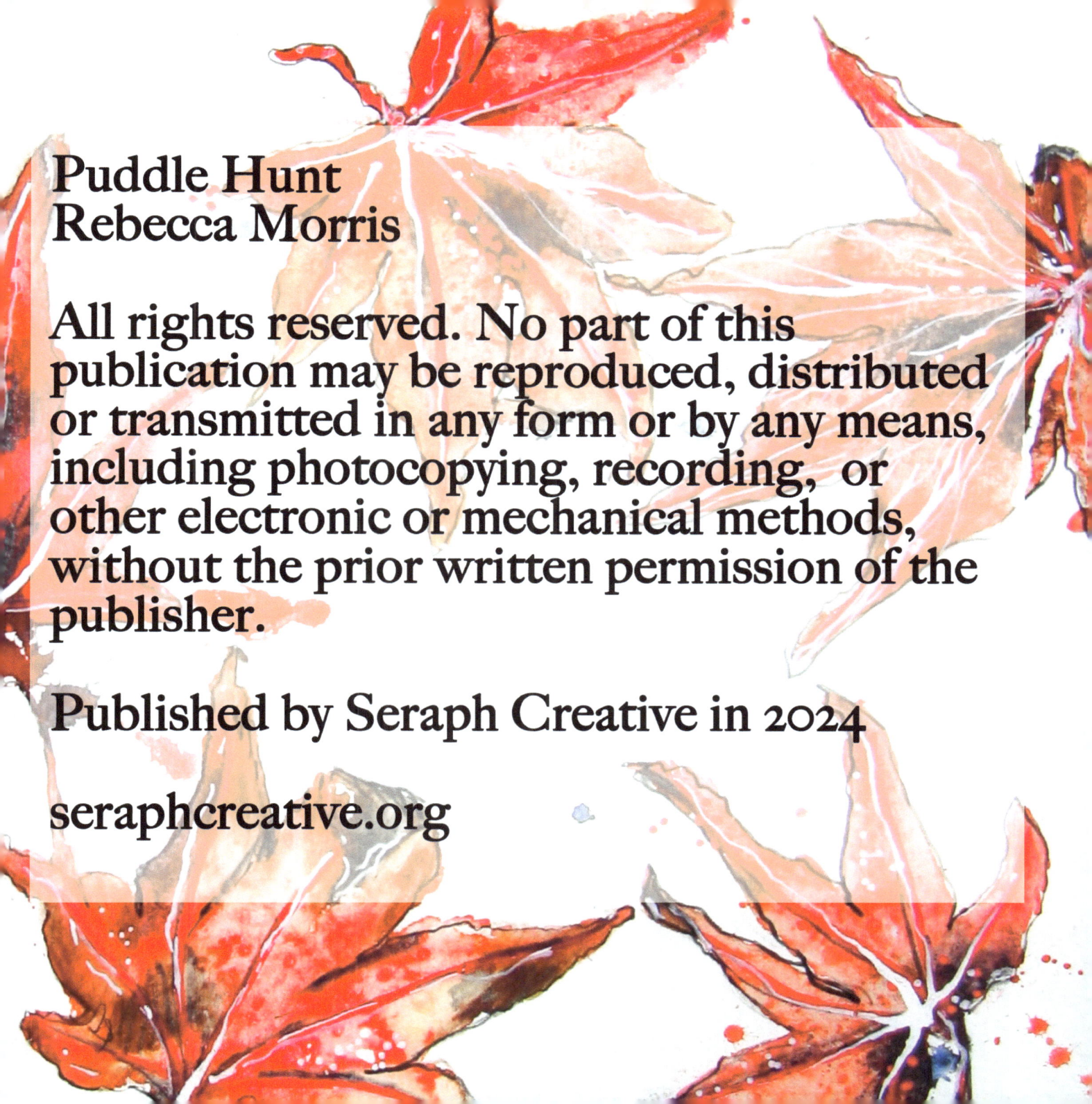

Puddle Hunt
Rebecca Morris

Published by Seraph Creative in 2024

seraphcreative.org

Seraph Creative is a collective of artists, writers, theologians & illustrators who desire to see the body of Christ grow into full maturity, walking in their inheritance as Sons Of God on the Earth.

Sign up to our newsletter to know about the release of the next book in the series, as well as other exciting releases.

Visit our website:
www.seraphcreative.org